I'm going to be the best astronaut ever!

One day I will go to astronaut school.

I will learn all about space.

I will learn to fly a rocket.

I will wear astronaut underwear.
Astronaut underwear looks like a big babysuit.
Tubes of liquid on the underwear hel
to keep me cool.

I will wear an astronaut's hat.

I'm going to be the Captain of a rocket.

3 . . . 2 . . . 1 . . .
blast off!
Me inside with
my crew
Really powerful
engines

Whoooooosh!
Really, really, hot flames

"Bye for now, everyone on Earth!"

I will look out of my window and I will see . . .

Earth, where I live

The Moon

A big rock called an asteroid. I hope it doesn't bash into my rocket!

Stars that
are very,
very far
away

Planets that
are different
colors
and sizes

Inside my rocket there will be lots of buttons and knobs.

I will know how to work everything.

I will be weightless, which means I will float around in my rocket.

I will have my own spacesuit.

It will have lots of pockets.

Me

It will protect me from harm in space.

Here are the things I am going to keep in my pockets.

Flashlight

Tools to fix my rocket

Space candy

Picture of my mom

I will put on my space helmet to go outside.

I will talk through my helmet radio.

I will go on a spacewalk.

This tube is
to stop me from
floating away.

"Hi!"

I might go outside
to fix my rocket.

I will visit a new Planet.
I will be very good at landing my rocket.
Space gloves
Space boots (very big and heavy)

I will go for a drive
in my space buggy.

My crew might
collect some
space rocks
to take home.

I might build a house in space.
I will grow a space garden.

I will eat space food.
It comes in tubes like toothpaste.
Me
I might meet a space alien.

When I get home I will be very famous.
I might be on TV.
Me

I might get a medal.
I might get my picture painted.
Me

Everyone will say I am the best astronaut ever!

Best in space

Me